3/97

Woodrow Wilson

Franklin D. Roosevelt

Harry S. Truman

EDMUND LINDOP

TWENTY-FIRST CENTURY BOOKS
A Division of Henry Holt and Company
New York

Twenty-First Century Books
A Division of Henry Holt and Company, Inc.
115 West 18th Street
New York, NY 10011

Henry Holt® and colophon are trademarks of
Henry Holt and Company, Inc.
Publishers since 1866
Text copyright © 1995 by Edmund Lindop
All rights reserved.
Published in Canada by Fitzhenry & Whiteside Ltd.
195 Allstate Parkway, Markham, Ontario L3R 4T8

Library of Congress Cataloging-in-Publication Data
Lindop, Edmund.
Woodrow Wilson, Franklin D. Roosevelt, Harry S. Truman / Edmund Lindop.
— 1st ed.
p. cm. — (Presidents who dared)
Includes bibliographical references and index,
1. Presidents—United States—Biography—Juvenile literature. 2. Wilson,
Woodrow, 1856–1924—Juvenile literature. 3. Roosevelt, Franklin D. (Franklin
Delano), 1882–1945—Juvenile literature. 4. Truman, Harry S., 1884–1972—
Juvenile literature. 5. United States—History—1901–1953—Juvenile litera-
ture. I. Title. II. Series.
E176.1.L529 1995
973'.099—dc20
[B]   95–19526
                                                      CIP
                                                      AC

ISBN 0–8050–3403–X
First Edition 1995
Printed in Mexico
All first editions are printed on acid-free paper ∞.
10 9 8 7 6 5 4 3 2 1

Cover design by Robin Hoffman
Interior design by Kelly Soong

Photo credits
Copyright by White House Historical Association,
photographs by National Geographic Society:
Cover (left) and p. 8: *Woodrow Wilson* by F. Graham Cootes
Cover (center) and p. 22: *Franklin D. Roosevelt* by Frank O. Salisbury
Cover (right) and p. 40: *Harry S. Truman* by Martha G. Kempton

For Alexander, Andrew, and Abigail Gebhart-Hardin

CONTENTS

This book discusses Woodrow Wilson, the twenty-eighth president; Franklin D. Roosevelt, the thirty-second president; and Harry S. Truman, the thirty-third president.

Woodrow Wilson, who became president in 1913, tried to keep the United States neutral in World War I. But Germany's continued attacks on American ships forced the United States to enter the conflict in 1917. After the fighting ended, President Wilson made a daring move—he proposed an international peacekeeping organization. The League of Nations was founded, but the U.S. Senate blocked the nation's participation in the league.

Franklin D. Roosevelt became president in 1933 in the midst of the worst economic depression in U.S. history. He dared to establish new agencies and programs to cope with the effects of the Great Depression. When the United States entered World War II in 1941, President Roosevelt led the nation with unwavering determination and emerged as the foremost leader of the free world.

Upon Roosevelt's death in office in 1945, Vice President Harry S. Truman became president. He will be forever remembered for his daring decision to drop atomic bombs on Japan in the hope of forcing a quick surrender. Later, President Truman took bold steps to contain the spread of communism.

1

WOODROW WILSON

Thomas Woodrow Wilson was born on December 28, 1856, in Staunton, Virginia. His father and one of his grandfathers were Presbyterian ministers. When Tommy was a year old, his father was hired to serve at a church in Augusta, Georgia, and the family moved to that city.

Tommy's earliest childhood memory was of a man standing at the gate of his house, shouting, "Mr. Lincoln's elected. There'll be a war."[1] The startled boy rushed into his house with the news, and his father sadly told him that a war between the North and the South probably would break out soon. President Lincoln, he explained, would resist the efforts of Southerners to set up a separate nation in which they could continue owning slaves.

When the Civil War began in April 1861, the Wilson family supported the Southern cause. Some of the soldiers who were injured in nearby battles were brought to Reverend Wilson's church, which served as a temporary hospital.

A frail and sickly child who had to wear glasses, Tommy was upset when he heard other youngsters in the neighborhood calling him a mama's boy. He also wasn't pleased when he heard adults say that he was a slow learner. Tommy was nine before he started school and was eleven before he could read well.

In 1873, when he was sixteen, Tommy was sent to Davidson College in North Carolina to prepare himself for the ministry. He earned good grades in most subjects and enjoyed being a member of the debating team and playing on the freshman baseball team. But poor health forced him to drop out of school at the end of his first year.

Tommy's life brightened in September 1875. By then his health had improved, and he enrolled at the College of New Jersey (now Princeton University). He studied hard but also found time for many extracurricular activities. Wilson wrote political articles for the school newspaper and became its editor in his senior year. He played an active role in the college debate club and eagerly argued political issues. Fascinated by sports, Wilson was the non-playing captain of the baseball team and president of the college football association—a position that gave him the opportunity to help coach the football team.

He also sang tenor in the college glee club, danced a spirited Scottish hornpipe, and was often called upon to tell humorous stories, which he did in various dialects. In college he decided to drop his first name and asked his friends to call him Woodrow instead of Tommy or Thomas.

Wilson's father had wanted his son to follow in his footsteps and become a minister. But by the time he was a college senior, Woodrow knew that his chief interests were politics and government service. So after college graduation he studied for a law degree at the University of Virginia and later practiced law briefly.

Soon Wilson discovered that he did not enjoy being a lawyer. Instead, he wanted to become a scholar and professor. In 1883 he began graduate work in political science at Johns Hopkins University in Baltimore, Maryland. While he was earning his Ph.D. (doctoral degree), he wrote a widely acclaimed book, *Congressional Government*. In this book Wilson argued that the United States too often has a weak president who allows Congress to dominate the government.

The same year that Wilson entered Johns Hopkins he met a beautiful woman, Ellen Louise Axson, the daughter of a Presbyterian minister in Rome, Georgia. Ellen was a delightful person who had a fondness for literature and music and was an excellent artist. The young couple became engaged, but they decided to postpone marriage until Woodrow had completed his studies and found a teaching position, which happened in 1885. The Wilsons had a happy marriage and had three daughters.

Woodrow's first teaching job was at Bryn Mawr, a new women's college in Pennsylvania. Later he taught history and political science at Wesleyan University in Connecticut, where he also organized a debating society and helped coach the football team. Then, in 1890, his alma mater, now known as Princeton, invited him to join its faculty.

For twelve years he taught at Princeton, becoming one of the school's most popular teachers. His classes were filled and students often applauded his lectures. Tall, lean, with a long face, blue-gray eyes, and a jutting jaw, Professor Wilson was a familiar sight as he pedaled his bicycle from home to his classroom. Rain or shine, during the football season he turned out daily for practices to teach the team new plays and correct any mistakes. He also wrote several brilliant books that brought him attention from scholars throughout the nation.

In 1902 forty-five-year-old Wilson became president

of Princeton—the school's first president who was not a minister. He vigorously started making reforms, reorganizing university departments and designing curriculum changes. Following the model of British colleges, he hired bright young teachers who would live in the student dormitories and act as tutors. President Wilson also proposed to abolish the private eating clubs for the sons of wealthy families and replace them with dining halls where students from all classes would take their meals together. This proposal was turned down by conservative alumni, but Wilson's standing with the public rose because the newspapers portrayed him as a fighter for democracy against the privileges of the rich.

In the spring of 1910 Wilson was called to a meeting of Democratic Party chieftains who asked him to run for governor of New Jersey. He agreed, but only if no strings were attached to the Democratic Party machine and no favors expected for party leaders. After receiving the nomination, he said, "For many years I have been preaching to the young men of Princeton that it was their duty to give service to the public and take their part in political affairs. This nomination has been handed to me on a silver platter, and I am under no obligations of any shape, manner, or form to anybody."[2]

Wilson was elected, and as New Jersey's new governor he coaxed the state legislature into passing one reform measure after another. To reduce the power of political bosses in selecting candidates, a law was passed providing that the people would vote in primary elections to nominate all elected officials in the state. Another new law set up a commission to protect citizens from unfair rates charged by public utilities, such as gas and electric companies. The state's first workers' compensation law was enacted; it provided payments to employees who were injured while working.

Even though he had served less than two years in an elected office, Wilson the reformer became a candidate for the Democratic nomination for president in 1912. Other candidates with much more political experience, including House of Representatives Speaker James "Champ" Clark, entered the race at the Democratic National Convention. Clark led in the early balloting, but he failed to acquire two-thirds of the delegates' votes, which was required to win the nomination. The weary delegates balloted forty-six times before finally selecting the former president of Princeton as their presidential nominee.

The 1912 election was an unusual contest: two Republicans were in the race for president. One was President William Howard Taft, running for a second term on the Republican ticket; the other was former President Theodore Roosevelt, the candidate of the Progressive (Bull Moose) Party.

Wilson campaigned on a program called the New Freedom. If elected, he promised to help the millions of people who again and again had been "knocking and fighting at the closed doors of opportunity."[3]

Wilson got only 42 percent of the popular vote, but he won the presidential election because the Republican vote was divided between the other two candidates. In the all-important electoral vote, he coasted to victory, gaining 435 votes to 88 for Roosevelt and only 8 for Taft. This was the only presidential election since the birth of the Republican Party in which its candidate finished in third place.

The new occupant of the White House believed that

the president should exercise strong leadership in dealing with Congress. Shortly after his inauguration, he appeared in person to deliver a message to Congress, the first president to do so since John Adams. (Thomas Jefferson, who had followed Adams into the presidency, was a poor speaker and sent written messages to Congress to be read by a clerk. Every later president followed Jefferson's tradition, until Wilson entered the office and chose to speak directly and forcefully to the lawmakers.)

Wilson skillfully maneuvered through Congress several major pieces of legislation. One of the bills dealt with the reduction of tariffs (taxes on imported goods) to make it possible for Americans to buy foreign products at cheaper prices. The bill passed quickly in the House of Representatives, but it stalled in the Senate because some businesses lobbied (tried to influence) senators to vote against it. President Wilson said "money without limit is being used to sustain this lobby. . . . Only public opinion can check and destroy it."[4] Senators soon were deluged by letters favoring the bill, and they voted to pass it.

The Underwood Tariff Act removed tariffs on iron, steel, wool, and sugar, and generally reduced tariffs on most other products by about 25 percent. This act also provided for a federal income tax in accord with the recently ratified Sixteenth Amendment to the Constitution. It placed a 1 percent tax on individual incomes above $3,000 and a tax of 6 percent on persons earning the highest incomes. (The average worker's yearly income in 1913 was $874.)

Next Wilson obtained the Federal Reserve Act, which brought about banking reforms and created twelve regional Federal Reserve banks governed by a board appointed by the president. In 1914 the Federal Trade Commission was established to guard against unfair business practices. The same year Wilson signed into law the Clayton Antitrust Act, which strengthened the government's power to prevent monopolies and protected laborers' rights to strike, picket, and boycott their employers.

In 1916 President Wilson nominated Louis Brandeis, a prominent Jewish attorney, to serve as a justice of the Supreme Court. As a lawyer, Brandeis had frequently attacked big business, and some conservatives charged that his ideas were radical. Despite powerful opposition, the Senate confirmed his appointment as the Supreme Court's first Jewish member.

In foreign affairs, Wilson faced some thorny problems that could not be resolved with the ease with which his New Freedom reforms were adopted by Congress. Civil war was raging in Mexico, and Victoriano Huerta, the leader of a Mexican army, had the president murdered, seized power, and set up a dictatorship. Wilson opposed Huerta's undemocratic regime. After some American sailors were arrested in a Mexican town, the U.S. president sent marines to occupy the Mexican port of Veracruz. Mexican revolutionaries forced Huerta to resign, and he was replaced by Venustiano Carranza.

When Wilson announced his approval of Carranza, this angered other rebel leaders, including the famous bandit-patriot Francisco "Pancho" Villa. Furious at American support of Carranza, Villa and a band of horsemen crossed the border and raided the town of Columbus, New Mexico, killing seventeen Americans. Wilson then ordered U.S. troops to invade northern Mexico and pursue Villa, but the elusive rebel chieftain was never captured.

An even more serious international crisis began in

Europe and developed into World War I. In August 1914 the Central Powers, led by Germany and Austria-Hungary, went to war against the Allied forces, or Allies, consisting mainly of Great Britain, France, and Russia. Wilson wanted to keep the United States out of this frightful conflict, and he urged American citizens to remain strictly neutral. Even so, he knew that future events might force the United States to enter the war.

In the same week that World War I started, Wilson was stricken by a personal tragedy. Kidney disease took the life of his beloved wife, Ellen. The president was nearly overcome with grief. Later he told a friend that he was not fit to be president because "he did not think straight any longer and had no heart for the things he was doing."[5] Wilson's three grown daughters tried to comfort their distraught father, but many months passed before he could shake off his gloom.

In March 1915 the president was introduced to Edith Bolling Galt, a Washington, D.C., widow who was a ninth-generation descendant of the American Indian Pocahontas and her English husband, John Rolfe. Friendship soon turned into romance. When Wilson discovered that Edith's favorite flower was the orchid, he sent her a fresh one every summer day. "You are the only woman I know who can wear an orchid," he wrote on a card. "On everybody else the orchid wears the woman."[6] Woodrow and Edith were married December 18, 1915.

Meanwhile, World War I was edging closer to American shores. "All the rest of the world is on fire," Wilson exclaimed, "and our own house is not fireproof."[7] Germans resented the United States loaning money and sending many products to the Allies. In May 1915 a German submarine torpedoed the British liner *Lusitania*, killing 1,200 people, including more than 120 American passengers. Other ships with Americans aboard were attacked, and Wilson protested these acts so vigorously that the Germans pledged to suspend unrestricted submarine warfare for a time.

As the 1916 presidential election approached, Wilson ran for a second term on the slogan "He Kept Us Out of War." His Republican opponent was Charles Evans Hughes, who had served as a justice of the Supreme Court and was a former governor of New York. With the Republicans united behind a single candidate—which had not been the case in 1912—the election was very close. The outcome was in doubt for two days until late returns from California gave that state and the election to Wilson.

In 1917, the fourth year of the war in Europe, Wilson's efforts to keep the United States out of the conflict no longer were successful. The Germans announced that starting February 1 they would sink without warning any ships, including American ships, engaged in trading with the Allies. Germany now appeared willing to risk war with the United States. This belief was strengthened when Americans intercepted a secret message in which Germany promised Mexico that it could take over Texas, Arizona, and New Mexico if it joined in fighting the United States. Mexico refused the German offer.

After German submarines began sinking American merchant ships, Wilson asked Congress to declare war. He told the lawmakers that Americans would fight "for the ultimate peace of the world . . . and for the privilege of men everywhere to choose their way of life. . . . The world must be made safe for democracy."[8] On April 6, 1917, Congress voted to declare war against the German aggressors.

A massive campaign to mobilize the United States produced a huge amount of war equipment and brought more than four million Americans into the armed forces, including almost two million who were sent to European battlefields. The president established special boards to regulate industry and transportation, and the people were asked to conserve food and fuel. Most Americans observed Meatless Mondays and Wheatless Wednesdays and reduced their use of fuel by wearing coats and sweaters in their homes on cold days.

Life in the White House was affected by the war, too. Entertaining was sharply restricted, and Edith Wilson sewed pajamas and knitted warm wool caps for the soldiers. To help free gardeners for war service, the Wilsons acquired a herd of sheep to graze on the vast White House lawn. The sheep kept the grass cut and, at shearing time, provided a large amount of wool. A nationwide auction of the White House wool brought in almost $100,000, which was donated to the war effort.

President Wilson was deeply concerned about what would be needed after the war to ensure a safe, peaceful world. In January 1918 he delivered to Congress his Fourteen Points speech in which he listed the goals that he believed America and the other Allies were fighting for. Among these goals were freedom of the seas, reduction of arms, removal of trade barriers, open instead of secret treaties, readjustment of European borders, and the fair division of lands claimed as colonies. The fourteenth point—the one that Wilson considered the most important—was the creation of a peacekeeping world organization, later known as the League of Nations. This organization was designed to ensure that no country ever again threatened the territory or independence of another country.

The tide of battle swung steadily in favor of the Allies in the summer and fall of 1918. The Germans retreated on every front, and on November 11, 1918, they surrendered. World War I was finally over—but at a devastating cost of over $300 billion and the tragic loss of more than 10 million lives, including more than 115,000 Americans.

The first American president to go to Europe while in office, Wilson helped to draft the peace treaty there. He appointed a group of advisers to accompany him but unwisely failed to include any prominent Republicans in the delegation. This proved to be a major mistake because the Republicans had won control of Congress in the 1918 elections and Wilson would need their support when the Senate voted on ratifying (approving) the peace treaty.

Before the treaty was drawn up, Wilson visited Paris, Rome, and London. In all three cities huge crowds cheered him wildly as the man with a plan for endless peace. Once the conference began, the president discovered that the leaders of France, Italy, and Britain were tough negotiators determined to punish Germany severely for the war losses that their countries had suffered. They opposed some of the Fourteen Points, and Wilson was forced to give up one point after another but refused to surrender his cherished idea of a League of Nations.

When the Treaty of Versailles, including provisions for the League of Nations, was completed, Wilson presented a copy to the Senate and urged its ratification. Senate Democrats generally favored the treaty. Senate Republicans were divided into two groups: a small number of them opposed the United States entrance into any world organization; a much larger group claimed they would support the League of Nations under certain conditions. They insisted on adding reservations, or amendments, to the treaty that would reserve the right of the United States to protect its freedom of action. They declared that, according to the Constitution, only Congress has the power to declare war and the League of Nations should not be permitted to force Americans to supply military aid to any nation without the approval of Congress.

Wilson was adamantly opposed to the idea that the United States membership in the league should be based on special favors and conditions that would not apply to other countries. Convinced that he could overwhelm his opponents by enlisting the public's support, the president decided to make a direct appeal to the people. Traveling from Ohio to the Pacific coast, he made thirty-seven speeches in twenty-two days on behalf of the league.

On his return trip the president addressed a cheering crowd in Pueblo, Colorado. With tears streaming down his cheeks, Wilson pleaded for the League of Nations as the only real hope of preventing future wars. That night he collapsed, and his train sped back to the nation's capital. A few days later he suffered a stroke that paralyzed his left side and left him bedridden for months.

In the Senate the fight over ratification of the Treaty of Versailles grew intense. The Democrats remained loyal to their president, but some of them believed it would be better to accept the Republicans' reservations than to let the treaty go down to defeat. Wilson stubbornly refused to compromise and sent word to the Democrats not to support the treaty if it contained the Republican amendments.

Twice the Senate voted on the treaty without the

Republican amendments, but both times it fell short of the two-thirds vote needed for ratification. The second time, on March 19, 1920, it received a majority of votes, forty-nine to thirty-five. If only seven more senators had voted for it, the treaty would have been ratified and the United States would have joined the League of Nations.

Edith Wilson tenderly cared for her husband during his long illness. To prevent him from becoming upset, she alone decided which letters and documents he could see. She also decided which visitors he could have and how long they could stay at his bedside. Some historians believe that Edith Wilson was an unofficial acting president for many months. Her role in making decisions angered some of her husband's opponents. "We have a petticoat government!" exclaimed one senator. "Mrs. Wilson is president!"[9]

The president recovered sufficiently to move around the White House in a wheelchair and to stand briefly with a cane. He and his wife went out for afternoon rides, but he had to be lifted into and out of the car.

After his presidential term ended in 1921, Wilson lived quietly with his wife in a house in Washington. He died on February 3, 1924, and was buried at the Washington Cathedral. His wife lived many more years, attended the inauguration of President John F. Kennedy in 1961, and died later that year at the age of eighty-nine.

In 1919 Woodrow Wilson predicted that if the United States did not join the League of Nations, the world organization would not be strong enough to prevent another devastating war. Twenty years later, when World War II began, his prophecy came true.

FRANKLIN D. ROOSEVELT

The only person in the history of the United States to be president for more than eight years was Franklin Delano Roosevelt, who held the office for a little more than twelve years. Roosevelt was elected to a third term of four years in 1940 and to a fourth term in 1944, but he died a few months after his final term began.

No future president will ever surpass Roosevelt's record for years served in the White House. In 1951 the Twenty-second Amendment, which prohibits a president from having more than two full terms, was added to the Constitution.

Franklin was born on January 30, 1882. His father, James Roosevelt, was a prosperous businessman who made his fortune in the railroad and coal industries. He traced his ancestry to a Dutch farmer who settled in what is now New York State about 1644. Franklin's mother, Sara Delano Roosevelt, was the daughter of a rich merchant involved in the trade between China and the United States.

Theodore Roosevelt, Franklin's fifth cousin, was a Republican, but James Roosevelt was a Democrat. In 1887 James took his five-year-old son to the White House to meet the Democratic president, Grover Cleveland. As he patted Franklin's blond head, the weary Cleveland told him, "My little man, I am making a strange wish for you. It is that you may never be president of the United States."[1]

An only child, Franklin had all the advantages that wealth and social position could provide. Surrounded by many servants, he lived in a large, comfortable house at Hyde Park, New York, along the Hudson River. At age four he was given a pony, at eleven his own hunting rifle, and at fourteen a twenty-one-foot sailboat. By the time he was fourteen, Franklin and his parents had taken eight long vacations in Europe.

While Franklin enjoyed many luxuries that most youngsters did not have, he also had some disadvantages. His doting parents pampered their son and denied him the freedom to plan his own activities, to make some mistakes, and to play with other children in the neighborhood whose families were not socially prominent. During his childhood young Roosevelt was taught at home by tutors and governesses. When he was fourteen his parents sent him to the fashionable Groton School, and he traveled to the campus in Massachusetts on his family's private railway car.

At Groton Franklin earned above-average but not outstanding grades. He plunged into extracurricular activities: singing in the choir, taking the role of an old country bumpkin in a school play, boxing, playing seventh-string on the football team, and serving as the manager of the baseball team. He also played on a baseball team called the Bum Baseball Boys, which he said was "made up of about the worst players in the school."[2] His one claim to athletic success was becoming the champion at a sport called the high kick; it required the performers to leap into the air and kick a tin pan suspended from the ceiling of the gym. Franklin was the best in his class and kicked the pan at a height of 7 feet 3½ inches—more than a foot higher than he stood.

After graduating from Groton, Franklin entered Harvard College, where he was only a fair student. Classes generally bored him, and he spent much of his time doing things that interested him. His favorite experience was editing the *Crimson*, Harvard's newspaper. Later he enrolled at Columbia Law School, but again classes bored him and he dropped out of school before earning his law degree. However, he studied on his own and passed the bar examination that allowed him to practice law.

While Franklin was attending Harvard, he began dating Anna Eleanor Roosevelt, a distant cousin and the favorite niece of President Theodore Roosevelt. Both of Eleanor's parents died while she was a child, and the young girl was sent to live with a stern, disapproving grandmother. Painfully shy and self-conscious, Eleanor was always "afraid of being scolded, afraid that other people would not like me."[3]

She was ashamed of her prominent nose, large, protruding teeth, shrill voice, and height—5 feet 10 inches. Eleanor was a "poor little thing," said her Aunt Edith. "She is very plain. Her mouth and teeth seem to have no future. But the ugly duckling may turn out to be a swan."[4]

Although Eleanor was no beauty, Franklin found her attractive. He was strongly impressed by her intelligence and enjoyed conversing with her on serious topics. She was very kind and expressed a deep sympathy for poverty-stricken people who daily faced hardships. And she had an inner strength that Franklin seemed to find reassuring.

Theodore Roosevelt gave Eleanor in marriage to Franklin on March 17, 1905. After kissing the bride, the president said, "Well, Franklin, there's nothing like keeping the name in the family!"[5]

Franklin shared more than his name with his famous cousin Teddy; the political careers of the two Roosevelts were strikingly similar. Both men first plunged into politics by being elected to the New York state legislature. (Franklin was the first Democrat in half a century to be elected state senator from his overwhelmingly Republican district.) Theodore was assistant secretary of the U.S. Navy when the Spanish-American War began; Franklin held this same position throughout World War I. Later in their careers both Roosevelts served as governor of New York before becoming president.

In 1920 Franklin was selected by the Democratic Party as its nominee for the vice presidency. The Democratic presidential candidate was Governor James M. Cox of Ohio, and his Republican opponent was Ohio Senator Warren G. Harding. Cox and Roosevelt fervently argued that the United States should enter the League of Nations that Woodrow Wilson, now at the end of his presidency, so strongly supported. But the voters, already weary from the sacrifices of World War I, were skeptical about their country's foreign affairs becoming entangled in any world organization. They elected Harding—who promised a "return to normalcy"—and his vice presidential running mate, Calvin Coolidge. Roosevelt was disappointed with the election results, but after campaigning in thirty-two states and addressing many large crowds, he had acquired a national reputation and felt his political future looked bright.

The amiable thirty-eight-year-old New Yorker had made many friends among his party's leaders. Standing 6 feet 1 inch tall, with blue eyes and dark wavy hair, Roosevelt was considered exceptionally handsome. He appeared strong and athletic and had a deep, commanding voice. And he belonged to one of America's most famous and favorite families.

The following summer, in 1921, something dreadful happened that appeared to mark the end of Roosevelt's promising political career. He was stricken with polio, or infantile paralysis. (At that time there was no vaccine for this disease.) His back, arms, and hands became partially paralyzed, and he lost the use of his legs.

His distraught mother demanded that her son accept that he was a hopeless cripple who always would stay inside his comfortable Hyde Park home, attended by nurses and servants. Franklin, however, refused to give up and spend the rest of his life as an invalid, and Eleanor agreed with her husband's decision.

Through ceaseless, painful exercises Franklin gradually improved. First he regained more movement of his fingers and hands. Then he worked on other parts of his body. In time he developed such powerful arms, shoulders, and chest muscles that the upper part of his body resembled that of a weight lifter.

For several years Roosevelt believed that with enough exercise he could regain the use of his legs, but they remained paralyzed. He did learn to walk again, although painfully, with the help of heavy steel leg braces and crutches. He spent most of his waking hours in a wheelchair and had to be lifted into and out of a car. Franklin was able to drive after he bought a specially built automobile that had all the controls on the dashboard.

In 1924 Roosevelt visited Warm Springs, a resort in

Georgia that had a pool with warm mineral waters. He was delighted with the pool because he could exercise his legs in its soothing waters. Franklin bought the resort and helped turn it into an international center for the study and treatment of infantile paralysis. He formed the nonprofit Warm Springs Foundation, which began attracting polio victims from many parts of the world.

As often as possible, Roosevelt returned to his cottage at Warm Springs, often accompanied by family members. He and Eleanor had one daughter, Anna, and four sons: James, Elliot, Franklin Jr., and John. (After World War II James became a congressman from California and Franklin Jr., a congressman from New York.)

Three years after his bout with polio began, Roosevelt returned to the political arena. At the 1924 Democratic National Convention he was scheduled to make a speech on behalf of New York Governor Alfred E. Smith, who was seeking the party's nomination for the presidency.

With a crutch under his left shoulder and clinging with his right arm to his son James, Roosevelt made his way slowly from the convention floor to the speaker's platform. Then, before a hushed audience, he slid his second crutch under his right shoulder and dragged his useless legs inch by inch to the speaker's stand. When he reached it, he dropped his crutches and gripped both sides of the stand. Sweating profusely from the ordeal, he tossed back his head and flashed the famous Roosevelt grin.

The spellbound spectators cheered long and loudly for the brave man who stood smiling before them. He gave a rousing speech for Smith, calling him the Happy Warrior, a nickname that would apply to the New York governor from then on. Smith did not win the presidential nomination, but Roosevelt achieved a personal triumph over the disease that had plagued him.

Four years later Smith tried again to win the Democratic Party's nomination for the presidency, and this time he was successful. Then he persuaded Roosevelt to run for the position he was vacating, governor of New York. Immediately some politicians and newspaper writers began complaining that Roosevelt was too crippled to hold such an active job as the state's chief executive. Smith replied sharply, saying that "a governor does not have to be an acrobat. We do not elect him for his ability to do a double back-flip or a handspring. The work of the governorship is brain work."[6]

Smith lost his 1928 bid for the presidency to Republican Herbert Hoover, but Roosevelt was narrowly elected governor of New York. The squire of Hyde Park established a progressive record as governor. He put the state finances in better order and coaxed the legislature to grant tax relief to farmers in economic difficulty. During his administration the workweek for women and children was reduced to forty-eight hours, workers' compensation for injuries on the job was increased, and improvements were made in state health care.

In October 1929 a sudden drop in the stock market greatly reduced the value of many companies' stocks and marked the beginning of the Great Depression. Soon businesses went bankrupt, factories closed, farmers lacked the money to make their mortgage payments, and millions of workers lost their jobs. Shortly after Roosevelt was reelected governor by a huge margin in 1930, he called the legislature into a special session to provide $20 million in relief to the unemployed—the first direct unemployment aid by any state.

As economic conditions worsened, many people blamed President Hoover for not taking strong enough action to deal with the grave problems caused by the Depression. Democratic Party chieftains felt confident that in the 1932 presidential election Hoover would be defeated in his bid for reelection and the Democrats would regain the White House after twelve years of Republican rule.

At the Democratic National Convention several prominent leaders contested for their party's presidential nomination. After balloting four times, the delegates selected Roosevelt as their presidential candidate. They named House Speaker John Nance Garner of Texas as their vice presidential candidate.

Traditionally, presidential nominees waited for the arrival of a committee to inform them officially of their nomination. Roosevelt announced that he was breaking this tradition. He would fly to Chicago, the site of the convention, to accept in person the nomination that his party had bestowed upon him. Commercial air travel was still in its infancy, and Roosevelt's flight from Albany, the New York state capital, to Chicago required two refueling stops and took nine hours.

The delegates grew weary waiting for the arrival of Roosevelt, who often was referred to by his initials, FDR. But their spirits soared when he entered the convention hall and addressed them eloquently. "I pledge you, I pledge myself," he said, "to a new deal for the American people. . . . Give me your help, not to win votes alone, but to win in this crusade to restore America to its own greatness."[7] At that time FDR gave no special significance to the words *new deal*, but soon they became the familiar motto of a whole new program of bold reforms.

The voters showed they were ready for a sweeping change in the leadership of their government. Roosevelt won in a landslide; Hoover carried only six states. Democrats also dominated Congress, which helped FDR to have the bills that he called for enacted into laws.

Between the time of his election and his inauguration, President-elect Roosevelt vacationed on a friend's yacht in the Bahamas. FDR went ashore in Miami and was driven in the backseat of an open car to a park where a large crowd waited to greet him. There he was joined in the car by Mayor Anton Cermak of Chicago.

As the two men were chatting, shots suddenly rang out. An unemployed bricklayer, Giuseppe Zangara, fired six bullets at Roosevelt. He failed to hit his target, but Cermak was shot and died. Zangara had come within inches of enormously changing the course of history. Later he claimed that he hated all presidents and rich people. Zangara was tried, convicted, and put to death in the electric chair.

Inauguration day, March 4, 1933, dawned cold and bleak. The nation's financial illness had become even more critical; bank after bank had been stripped of its resources and had to close its doors. Millions of frightened, desperate people—some not knowing when they would get their next meal or have a roof over their heads—listened on radios to their new president's message.

"This great nation will endure as it has endured, will revive and prosper," FDR assured the people. "So first of all, let me assert my firm belief that the only thing we have to fear is fear itself." The president stressed the need for prompt, bold, decisive action. He warned that if Congress failed to take such action he would not hesitate to ask for broad executive power "to wage a war against the emergency, as great as the power that would be given to me if we were in fact invaded by a foreign foe."[8]

The inaugural address was better than any tonic for stirring fresh hope and courage in the hearts of the American people. In the next week almost half a million letters poured into the White House, praising the new president for his promise to act quickly.

The day after he took office Roosevelt ordered a national bank holiday until Congress could set up effective regulations for the banking system. A few days later Congress passed an emergency banking bill that laid down the conditions under which the banks could be reopened. At the end of his first week in office, the president spoke to the nation in the first of his many radio "fireside chats." He promised that the banks would be reopened as soon as they met certain standards, and within a few weeks three-fourths of the nation's banks were in operation again.

During Roosevelt's first term in the White House many New Deal programs and agencies were launched. Unemployment was the most pressing problem, and the Federal Emergency Relief Administration (FERA) gave money to the states and cities for unemployment relief. Later the president decided it would be better if the federal government provided jobs for the unemployed and paid them wages for their work. The Works Progress Administration (WPA) was created. In addition to hiring a huge army of construction workers, the WPA also gave jobs to thousands of unemployed writers, artists, actors, and musicians. Thousands of schools, hospitals, and highways were built during this time, some of which are still in use today.

The Agricultural Adjustment Act (AAA) was passed to bring the farmers more income by reducing crop surpluses and paying farmers to limit their crops. The Tennessee Valley Authority (TVA) improved living conditions by promoting better use of natural resources in the vast Tennessee Valley, which includes parts of seven states. The TVA harnessed the floodwaters of the Tennessee River and its tributaries through the construction of giant dams. These dams also furnished cheap electricity to an area where only two out of every one hundred families previously had electric lights and power.

The Civilian Conservation Corps (CCC) employed more than 2.5 million young men to work in the outdoors, planting trees, carving out trails and firebreaks, and building bridges and reservoirs. Congress established the National Recovery Administration (NRA) to help revive the nation's businesses and the Securities and Exchange Commission (SEC) to correct the abuses that had led to the stock market crash in 1929. The National Labor Relations Act required employers to bargain with unions representing the majority of workers in their industry.

Of all the New Deal reform measures, perhaps the most significant was the establishment of Social Security in 1935. This system provides old-age pensions for retired workers, insurance for unemployed persons, and benefits for the survivors of workers who have died and for physically disabled persons.

Women played an important role in the Roosevelt administration. FDR appointed the first female envoy to a foreign country, the first woman judge of the U.S. Court of Appeals, and the first woman member of a president's cabinet—Secretary of Labor Frances Perkins. And the First Lady assisted her husband in many ways. Eager to learn firsthand about social and economic concerns, Eleanor Roosevelt provided the eyes and ears for the crippled president. She personally visited the soot-laden coal mines, the unsafe factories, the run-down farms, and the poverty-stricken slums to find out the needs of the people. Then she reported what she had discovered to the president and to the nation in numerous press conferences and in a newspaper column called "My Day."

In foreign affairs, Roosevelt wanted to improve relations with the other countries in the Western Hemisphere. He supported a policy whereby all the American nations would respect one another as equals. The Good Neighbor policy ushered in an era of much closer ties between the United States and the Latin American countries.

In the 1936 presidential election FDR ran for a second term. Winning all but two states, he easily routed Republican Alfred M. Landon. His victory was by a larger margin than that of any presidential candidate since 1820 when James Monroe had no opponent.

Roosevelt's administration, however, had some outspoken critics. They charged that the president had seized too much power for himself and the federal government. They portrayed the New Deal, with its numerous agencies and huge army of federal employees, as a monstrous octopus intent on strangling the individual's self-reliance and initiative. Many people were distressed that the government could not balance its budget and kept raising taxes to finance its programs.

The New Deal faced opposition on another front, too. Both the NRA and the AAA had been declared unconstitutional by the Supreme Court. This angered Roosevelt, who feared that other New Deal projects might also be struck down by the Court. So, in February 1937, he proposed to Congress a plan to add one extra justice for every justice over seventy who refused to retire. Because there were then six justices on the Supreme Court over seventy, the president could appoint six additional members— probably all New Deal supporters—if none of the older justices retired.

Traditionally, the Supreme Court was considered an unbiased umpire that decided cases without being partial to either side. Many people protested FDR's Court-packing plan as an attempt to unfairly "fix [influence] the umpire." The Senate turned down the measure by a large margin of votes, and this marked the first time that a house of Congress had rebuked the president on a major issue.

During the late 1930s Roosevelt had to turn his attention mainly to international problems. In Europe and Asia aggressor nations threatened a second world war. The German Nazis under dictator Adolf Hitler took over neighboring Austria and Czechoslovakia. Italian Fascist leader Benito Mussolini gobbled up helpless Ethiopia in Africa. A militant regime in Japan was conquering China and threatening all of Southeast Asia. Not knowing where or when the dictators would strike again, Britain and France began rearming frantically.

The United States was legally bound not to help Britain and France. Between 1935 and 1937 Congress had passed neutrality acts that banned the sale and transportation of munitions to countries preparing for war.

As the prospects of war increased, Roosevelt tried to persuade Congress to repeal the arms embargo. "The world has grown so small and weapons of attack so swift, that no nation can be safe," he told Congress in January 1939. "There are methods short of war . . . of bringing home to aggressor governments the . . . sentiments of our people."[9]

It was not until World War II began in September 1939 with the German invasion of Poland that Congress finally agreed to end the arms embargo. The fall of France and the relentless bombing of Britain in 1940 drew the United States even closer to Britain. Although the United States was still technically neutral, in September 1940 FDR announced plans to deliver to the British fifty old destroyers in exchange for some naval and air bases in Canada and Latin America.

In the midst of this international tension the 1940 presidential election occurred. Like a good soldier, FDR felt he must not desert his post. Republicans cried out "no third term," while Democrats insisted that leaders "should not be changed in midstream." Roosevelt defeated Republican Wendell Willkie, but not by as large a margin as he had won in his first two presidential elections.

Roosevelt persuaded Congress in March 1941 to pass the Lend-Lease Act, under which the United States would lend or lease military equipment to Britain. Military equipment also was sent to the Soviet Union after it was attacked by Germany in June 1941. The United States became the "great arsenal of democracy," and during the remainder of the war it shipped to the Allies weapons and supplies valued at nearly $50 billion.

In August 1941 Roosevelt and British Prime Minister

Winston Churchill met on shipboard off the coast of Newfoundland and jointly issued the Atlantic Charter. Somewhat similar to Woodrow Wilson's Fourteen Points, the Atlantic Charter set forth goals to be achieved in the postwar world. It said that people everywhere should have the right to choose their own form of government and be entitled to the Four Freedoms—freedom of speech, freedom of religion, freedom from want, and freedom from fear.

During the summer and fall of 1941 German submarines attacked American ships in the Atlantic Ocean, but it was an act of treachery by Japan in the Pacific Ocean that forced the United States into the world conflict. Early in the morning of December 7, 1941, Japanese planes bombarded the American military base at Pearl Harbor in Hawaii. Besides destroying or damaging many warships in the harbor and many warplanes on the ground, the Japanese sneak attack killed about 2,400 Americans and wounded another 1,200.

President Roosevelt grimly addressed Congress, declaring that December 7 was "a date which will live in infamy [disgrace]."[10] Soon the United States was deeply involved in a difficult two-front war against Japan in Asia and Germany and Italy in Europe. Millions of courageous Americans fought valiantly, with more than 400,000 of them sacrificing their lives. Millions of other Americans on the home front worked around the clock to build an astounding number of planes, ships, and other war products.

For most of 1942 the aggressors were advancing on several fronts, but by the end of the year the Allies slowly began to turn the tide. The German invasions of the Soviet

Union and North Africa were halted, and Americans defeated Japanese fleets in the battles of Coral Sea and Midway. During 1943 and 1944 American and British forces moved into Italy, while other Americans were liberating Pacific islands that had been seized by Japan. On June 6, 1944, D day, Allied troops landed on the coast of France at Normandy, and by September they had reached the western boundary of Germany.

Throughout the war FDR had meetings with Churchill and Soviet leader Joseph Stalin. They discussed military strategy and also helped lay the groundwork for a new world organization, the United Nations.

The enormous strain that came from shouldering duties as the foremost leader of the free world sapped FDR's strength and weakened his health. But because he did not want to leave his job unfinished, Roosevelt ran for a fourth term in 1944 and defeated Republican Thomas E. Dewey, governor of New York. Senator Harry S. Truman of Missouri became the nation's vice president.

On April 12, 1945, the president was going over some papers in his cottage at Warm Springs while an artist was painting his portrait. Suddenly he said, "I have a terrific headache."[11] Losing consciousness, he slumped over in his chair, the victim of a cerebral hemorrhage. While a grief-stricken nation mourned his passing, he was buried at Hyde Park.

Roosevelt died less than two weeks before the charter creating the United Nations was drafted. On May 7 the Germans surrendered, and in September the Japanese also surrendered. The world's most devastating war had finally ended.

Even though he did not live to see his work completed, Franklin D. Roosevelt had bright hopes for the future. The last words that he had written on the day of his death were: "The only limit to our realization of tomorrow will be our doubts of today. Let us move forward with strong and active faith."[12]

3

HARRY S. TRUMAN

When their first son was born May 8, 1884, at the family home in Lamar, Missouri, John and Martha Truman named him Harry after an uncle, Harrison Young. For his middle name they considered Shippe, the name by which his grandfather Anderson Shippe Truman was known, and also Solomon, the name of his other grandfather, Solomon Young. But since they did not want to show favoritism, Harry's parents selected the letter S to honor both grandfathers. This single letter was the boy's full middle name.

John Truman, Harry's father, was a livestock trader and farmer in western Missouri. Harry's mother, Martha Young Truman, grew up in a Missouri family that strongly supported the South during the Civil War. Martha was briefly imprisoned by Northern soldiers, and for the rest of her life she never forgave President Abraham Lincoln and the North for this humiliating experience. (When she visited the White House after her son became president, Mrs. Truman said she would rather spend the night on the floor than sleep in Lincoln's bed.)

In 1890 the Truman family moved to the town of Independence, Missouri, a few miles east of Kansas City. There Harry, along with his younger brother, Vivian, and his younger sister, Mary Jane, attended elementary school and high school.

From an early age Harry had to wear expensive glasses with thick lenses. This prevented him from taking part in most sports and other physical activities. "I was so carefully cautioned by the eye doctor about breaking my glasses and injuring my eyes," he said, "that I was afraid to join in the rough-and-tumble games in the schoolyard and back lot."[1]

While the other boys in his neighborhood were playing outdoors, Harry was spending many hours reading the books in the town library. He claimed that by the time he was fourteen he had read every one of the library's two thousand books. Harry especially enjoyed reading books about history. He later said that "reading history, to me, was far more than a romantic adventure. It was solid instruction and wise teaching which I somehow felt that I wanted and needed."[2] After he became president, he often drew on his wide knowledge of history before making important decisions.

Playing the piano was another of young Harry's chief interests. He usually practiced classical numbers—mainly the works of Mozart, Chopin, and Bach—for two hours before going to school. After a recital he gave at the age of fourteen, a newspaper reviewer predicted that he would achieve musical fame. Many years later, while he was president, Harry gave a famous conductor his picture with this inscription: "From Harry Truman, who almost became a pianist."[3]

About the time that Harry graduated from high school, his father suffered severe financial losses, and Harry had to go to work to help support his younger brother and sister, in addition to himself. He got a job working as an accountant for crews building the Santa Fe Railroad. Later he became a bank clerk, then a bookkeeper.

Although Harry dreamed of going to college, his family had no funds for this and needed the money he could earn. He sought an appointment to the U.S. Military Academy at West Point, where his expenses would be paid by the government, but he was turned down because of his poor eyesight. (Harry Truman was the only president in the twentieth century who had no college education.)

In 1906, when Truman was twenty-two, his father asked him to go to Grandview, Missouri, to take charge of his grandmother's farm. For the next eleven years Harry toiled in the fields, raising corn, cattle, and hogs for sale and vegetables and chickens for family meals.

If the United States had not been drawn into World War I in 1917, Truman might never have left the farm. He had joined the Missouri National Guard in 1905, and when America went to war, his unit was mobilized as part of the regular army. Truman served with the 129th Field Artillery. Shortly after he landed in France, the Missouri farmer was given command of Battery D, which engaged in heavy fighting against the Germans. During the war Truman rose in rank from lieutenant to major.

Shortly after returning home, Truman married his childhood sweetheart, Elizabeth Wallace, whom everyone called Bess. Harry was six years old when he first met Bess at Sunday school. They went through elementary and high school together. Harry described Bess as "the prettiest, sweetest little girl I'd ever seen" and said, "If I succeeded in carrying her books to school or back home for her I had a big day."[4]

Bess was a good athlete, winning first place in the shot put at a school track meet. She also excelled at tennis and baseball. While Harry could only umpire baseball games because of his glasses, Bess played well in the infield and was a powerful hitter.

The couple became engaged before Harry joined the army, but fearing that he might be killed in a battle, he insisted that they wait until the war ended before they married. Harry was thirty-five and Bess thirty-four when they married. They had one daughter, Margaret, who pursued a career as an opera singer and later became a writer.

Harry and Bess lived at her mother's home in Independence, while he and an army buddy opened a men's clothing store in nearby Kansas City. At first the store profited, but as prices for farm products began dropping drastically in 1921, farmers no longer could afford to buy fancy silk shirts and expensive neckties. After Truman had lost about $30,000, the store had to be closed in 1922. Some investors who went broke during the period of declining farm prices declared bankruptcy to avoid paying off all their debts. But Truman vowed to pay back every dollar he owed, and he did, even though it took him fifteen years.

Jim Pendergast, another of Truman's army buddies, was the nephew of Tom Pendergast, who headed a powerful political machine in Kansas City. At that time political machines were common in large cities, and their bosses usually selected their own candidates for offices and helped them win elections. Illegal means were sometimes used to secure victory for machine candidates: these practices included stuffing ballot boxes with the votes of dead persons and with the ballots of people who voted more than once. In return, the victorious machine candidates were expected to do favors for the bosses, often including making arrangements that allowed companies to secure government contracts by paying bribes to the heads of political machines.

When Jim Pendergast described Truman as a loyal, hardworking, very intelligent man, the Pendergast machine in 1922 offered him the opportunity to run for one of the three county judgeships in Jackson County, Missouri. By this time Truman had acquired a strong desire to enter politics, but he was unknown to most voters. He had no money to spend on a campaign and needed the help of some strong political group to stand a chance of winning any election. So he accepted the support of the Pendergast machine, although he had no intention of doing anything dishonest as a favor for the machine—and he never did.

Truman won this election, but becoming a county judge in Missouri did not mean that he would preside over a court of law. The three-man board of judges in Jackson County was responsible for constructing and maintaining roads, highways, bridges, parks, and public institutions such as hospitals and orphanages.

In 1924 Truman was defeated for reelection, largely because of strong opposition by the Ku Klux Klan. The Klan falsely portrayed him as being partly Jewish and was angered when he bluntly refused its demand that he not hire Catholics in his office. (The Ku Klux Klan, an organization that considers all racial and religious minorities as inferior, was powerful in some states in the 1920s.)

In 1926 Truman was elected to a higher position—presiding judge of Jackson County. He spent the next eight years reducing the government debt, fighting corruption, supervising the construction of new public institutions, and building a network of highways and roads that profited both farmers and businesses in his region.

Much to Judge Truman's surprise, in 1934 Tom Pendergast asked him to run for a seat in the United States Senate. Truman's greatest challenge was winning the Democratic primary election, since two well-known members of the House of Representatives also were seeking the Democratic nomination for the Senate. The plucky former farmer rolled up his sleeves and waged a strenuous campaign, speaking in countless towns and even tiny hamlets. He captured the Democratic nomination and then easily defeated his Republican opponent in the general election.

When fifty-year-old Harry Truman moved his family to the nation's capital, he did not receive a warm welcome from many of the other senators. They suspected that he was nothing more than the puppet of the corrupt Pendergast machine, and some colleagues even slyly referred to him as the "senator from Pendergast." As time passed, however, Truman proved that he was an honest, dedicated public servant who took orders from no boss except the American people. Gradually his ceaseless energy, wise judgment, fairness to everyone, and friendly manner made him one of the most popular members of the Senate.

Tom Pendergast was sent to prison in 1939 for his corrupt dealings, and the political machine he had headed was stripped of its power. The following year Senator Truman sought reelection with no robust political organization to support him. In the Democratic primary he had two strong rivals, Governor Lloyd Stark and Maurice Milligan, the U.S. attorney who had prosecuted Pendergast. Having almost no money for billboards and radio ads, Truman set out in his car and drove into seventy-five Missouri counties to talk to the voters personally. He told them that he vigorously supported the economic policies established by President Franklin D. Roosevelt to help the common people at a time when so many were in desperate need of government assistance. "I was a New Dealer from the start," he proudly proclaimed.[5]

Truman narrowly won the Democratic primary by about eight thousand votes. In the fall election he defeated his Republican opponent by nearly forty-five thousand votes. On the same day in 1940 when Truman was reelected to the Senate, Roosevelt won a third term in the White House.

World War II was then engulfing Europe, and the United States was trying to rearm quickly. The scramble to build defense plants, ships, planes, and bases for the armed forces was resulting in a huge waste of money and raw materials. Truman became keenly aware of this deplorable situation when he visited many defense installations during his 1940 reelection campaign. After he returned to Washington he convinced Congress to set up the Special Committee to Investigate the National Defense Program. The committee's purpose was to make sure that every tax dollar spent for the defense effort brought a full dollar's worth of war materials.

Senator Truman headed this committee, which launched investigations of many factories and armed-forces bases throughout the country. Its work took on added importance after the United States entered the war in December 1941 and had to fight Germany and Italy in Europe and Japan in Asia. By the end of the war it was estimated that the Truman committee had saved the government about $15 billion. A survey of Washington newspaper correspondents showed that they regarded Truman second only to Roosevelt as the man in government who had contributed most to the war effort.

When Roosevelt sought a fourth term as president, he lacked his usual vigor and appeared ill and weary. Politicians speculated that if he were elected again he might not live to complete his term, and the vice president then would be elevated to the presidency. Several Democratic Party leaders were eager to be selected as the vice presidential nominee, but not Truman, who said he was happy to remain a senator. President Roosevelt, however, convinced Truman to be his running mate, and the Democratic candidates defeated their Republican rivals in the 1944 general election.

Eighty-two days after Truman was sworn in as vice president, Roosevelt died. FDR had talked with his vice president only a few brief times and had failed to tell him about the government's pressing problems and major plans, including the development of the atomic bomb. With virtually no information from the man he followed into the White House, the former farmer from Missouri suddenly had thrust upon him the most important job in the world!

The day after Roosevelt's death Truman said to reporters, "Boys, when they told me yesterday what had happened, I felt like the moon and stars and all the planets had fallen on me. . . . If you fellows ever pray, pray for me now."[6]

The new president took office on April 12, 1945, and his first big decision was whether the international conference to write a charter forming the United Nations would still begin April 25 in San Francisco, California. Yes, he announced, the UN conference would go ahead as planned. "I did not hesitate a second," he later explained. "It was of supreme importance that we build an organization to help keep the future peace of the world."[7]

The Germans surrendered in May, but the United States still had to contend with the Japanese armed forces. When President Truman learned in July that the first test of the atomic bomb at Alamogordo, New Mexico, had been successful, he had to decide whether to use this new weapon—by far the most devastating that the world had ever known—against the Japanese. He realized that it could cause enormous destruction and the loss of many lives. Still, he felt that the only other course of action was an invasion of Japan, which would have pitted about one million Americans against a Japanese force of about two million troops. Such an invasion could have resulted in hundreds of thousands of casualties on both sides.

President Truman gave the command to unleash the first atomic bombs. One target was Japan's industrial city of Hiroshima. When the bomb struck Hiroshima on August 6, 1945, about 80,000 people were immediately burned to death, and in the months and years that followed, many thousands more died from the effects of radiation. Three days later a second bomb was dropped on Nagasaki, causing about 70,000 more deaths. The Japanese government then surrendered in September.

Accepting full responsibility for the use of these powerful weapons, Truman justified his action as the only means of preventing many more casualties if the war dragged on. "I wanted to save half a million boys on our side," he said, "and as many on their side. I never lost any sleep over my decision."[8]

On the home front the president proposed a series of reform measures known as the Fair Deal—a continuation and expansion of FDR's New Deal. The Fair Deal succeeded in providing federal funds for slum clearance and new housing. It extended Social Security to cover many more people and increased the minimum (lowest) wage to 75¢ an hour from the 40¢ set in 1940. It also desegregated the armed forces by executive order.

Some other parts of the Fair Deal were rejected by Congress. The president was unable to obtain laws ending the payment of poll taxes in federal elections or banning segregation in interstate transportation. Congress refused to establish a permanent Fair Employment Practices Commission to protect the rights of minorities in the workplace. Lawmakers also blocked his proposal for government-sponsored medical insurance.

Foreign events caused Truman his gravest concerns. The alliance that had bound the Soviets, Americans, and British together during World War II began coming apart in the postwar world. The Soviet Union broke its pledge to allow free elections in the countries of Eastern Europe that it had freed from German rule. Instead, the Soviets turned these nations into puppet states answering to Soviet directions. An "iron curtain" of Communist domination fell over Eastern Europe. This marked the beginning of a dangerous "cold war" between communism and democracy that would last for nearly half a century.

Greece and Turkey still were free, but in 1947 the Soviets tried to extend their control to these two nations. President Truman then went before Congress and firmly declared, "I believe that it must be the policy of the United States to support free peoples who are resisting attempted subjugation [conquest]."[9] Congress responded to his call and voted to spend money to enforce the president's policy to save Greece and Turkey from Communist takeovers—a policy that came to be known as the Truman Doctrine.

In 1947 Secretary of State George C. Marshall announced plans to extend the Truman Doctrine to rebuild Europe from the ashes of World War II. The following year Congress approved the Marshall Plan, which could have included the Soviet Union, but it refused to participate. Soon the United States began sending billions of dollars to help the countries of Western Europe restore healthy economies.

The Soviets stubbornly refused to agree with their former allies about the future of defeated Germany. Eventually it became two countries—West Germany, which was free and democratic, and East Germany, which was Communist-controlled. The city of Berlin lay about one hundred miles inside Communist East Germany, and it also was divided into two sections—Communist East Berlin and free West Berlin. In 1948 the Communists closed all the highways, railroads, and river routes that ran from West Germany into West Berlin. They thought that when the West Berliners could no longer get food and fuel from West Germany they would surrender their freedom.

The Communists, however, had not reckoned with the determination of the American president to keep West Berlin free. Truman ordered the launching of a dangerous airlift that would fly huge amounts of vital supplies to West Berliners. He knew that he was risking war with the Soviet Union if the American planes were attacked. But the

Communists did not challenge the Berlin airlift, and nearly a year later they lifted their siege of the city.

President Truman again demonstrated courage and decisiveness after the establishment of the Jewish nation of Israel in 1948. Some of his advisers cautioned the president that American recognition of this new nation could lead to troubles with its Arab neighbors. But the president believed that the Jews were entitled to a homeland, and his recognition of their nation paved the way for establishing close relations between the United States and Israel.

When Truman ran for another presidential term in 1948, he faced three strong rivals. The Republicans nominated Thomas E. Dewey, the popular governor of New York. The Democratic Party was splintered into three groups. Truman was the candidate of the regular party members. But some liberals who believed that the president was being too tough on the Communists nominated Henry Wallace, a former vice president, on the Progressive Party ticket. Some southerners who opposed Truman's strong stand in favor of more civil rights for minorities supported Strom Thurmond of South Carolina, the candidate of the States' Rights (Dixiecrat) Party.

The polls and the political experts all predicted that Truman would lose the election to Dewey by a large margin of votes. But, unruffled by the enormous odds against him, the battling president embarked on a long railroad whistle-stop campaign and spoke to about six million cheering people. His speeches were homely, down-to-earth, hard-hitting talks about the failure of the Republican-dominated Congress to pass bills needed by average Americans. When the votes were counted, Truman had won the most astonishing upset victory in the history of presidential elections.

In his inaugural address on January 20, 1949, President Truman proposed that the United States extend its aid to the "more than half of the people of the world . . . living in conditions approaching misery."[10] He called for a Point Four program designed to provide underdeveloped countries with financial assistance and technical training needed to improve their economies. Congress approved the Point Four program and voted to spend large amounts of money to help underprivileged people in many parts of the world.

In 1949 the United States joined nine European countries, Canada, and Iceland to form a military alliance called the North Atlantic Treaty Organization (NATO). Under the NATO agreement each country was bound to treat an attack on one member as an attack on all. For the first time in its history the United States had made an alliance in peacetime, and Europe now became America's first line of defense.

The Communists did not test the strength of NATO in Europe, but they did strike in another part of the world. In 1950 the Communist government of North Korea launched a full-scale attack on South Korea. President Truman ordered American forces into battle as the United Nations Security Council—with the Soviet Union boycotting its sessions—called on all UN members to defend South Korea against the aggressors.

A lengthy struggle followed. UN troops, chiefly Americans and South Koreans, at first were forced to retreat. Later they mounted an offensive, driving the aggressors back into North Korea and almost to the border between that nation and Communist China. Suddenly a huge horde of Chinese soldiers entered North Korea and began pushing the UN forces back. The Chinese finally were halted near the border between the two Koreas, where the fighting had begun.

Truman did not want to risk enlarging the Korean War into a major conflict with Communist China and possibly the Soviet Union, which was supplying North Korea with military equipment. When General Douglas MacArthur, commander of the UN forces, disagreed with this policy and made statements calling for military action against China, the president stripped MacArthur of his command. The Korean War ended in 1953, shortly after Truman left the presidency, with the Communists unable to claim victory over the country they had invaded.

The former president retired to Independence, Missouri, where he wrote his memoirs and supervised the construction of the Truman Library and Museum. He died in 1972 at the age of eighty-eight and was buried in the courtyard behind the library. Bess Truman outlived her husband by ten years, dying at the age of ninety-seven. She had the longest life of any First Lady.

Harry Truman always was proud to have been a farmer, a soldier, and an honest politician who never shied away from making tough decisions and who worked tirelessly for the American people. "History justifies the honorable politician when he works for the welfare of the country," he said. "More young men and women should fit themselves for politics and government."[11]

SOURCE NOTES

1

1. Doris Faber and Harold Faber, *Great Lives: American Government* (New York: Scribners, 1988), 163.

2. Alice Osinski, *Woodrow Wilson* (Chicago: Childrens Press, 1989), 42.

3. Frank Freidel, *Our Country's Presidents* (Washington, D.C.: National Geographic Society, 1981), 233.

4. David C. Whitney, *The American Presidents* (Garden City, N.Y.: Doubleday, 1985), 233.

5. August Heckscher, *Woodrow Wilson* (New York: Scribners, 1991), 341.

6. James Cross Giblin, *Edith Wilson: The Woman Who Ran the United States* (New York: Viking, 1992), 16.

7. Freidel, *Our Country's Presidents*, 170.

8. Osinski, *Woodrow Wilson*, 75.

9. Rhoda Blumberg, *First Ladies* (New York: Franklin Watts, 1981), 38.

2

1. Nathan Miller, *FDR: An Intimate History* (Garden City, N.Y.: Doubleday, 1983), 22.

2. Edmund Lindop and Joseph Jares, *White House Sportsmen* (Boston: Houghton Mifflin, 1964), 25.

3. Russell Freedman, *Franklin Delano Roosevelt* (New York: Clarion Books, 1990), 27.

4. Arden Davis Melick, *Wives of the Presidents* (Maplewood, N.J.: Hammond, 1985), 70.

5. Doris Faber, *Eleanor Roosevelt: First Lady of the World* (New York: Viking Penguin, 1985), 19.

6. John W. Selfridge, *Franklin D. Roosevelt: The People's President* (New York: Fawcett Columbine, 1990), 66.

7. Miller, *FDR*, 279.

8. Freedman, *Franklin Delano Roosevelt*, 88.

9. Ted Morgan, *FDR: A Biography* (New York: Simon and Schuster, 1985), 502.

10. Joseph Alsop, *FDR, 1882–1945: A Centenary Remembrance* (New York: Viking, 1982), 213.

11. Jim Bishop, *FDR's Last Year: April 1944–April 1945* (New York: Morrow, 1974), 531.

12. Whitney, *The American Presidents*, 277.

3

1. Jim Hargrove, *Harry S. Truman* (Chicago: Childrens Press, 1987), 23.

2. David G. McCullough, *Truman* (New York: Simon and Schuster, 1992), 58.

3. Edmund Lindop and Joy Crane Thornton, *All About Democrats* (Hillside, N.J.: Enslow, 1985), 19.

4. Melick, *Wives of the Presidents*, 74.

5. McCullough, *Truman*, 219.

6. Donald E. Cooke, *Atlas of the Presidents* (Maplewood, N.J.: Hammond, 1977), 79.

7. Whitney, *The American Presidents*, 283.

8. Morrie Greenberg, *The Buck Stops Here: A Biography of Harry Truman* (Minneapolis: Dillon Press, 1989), 75.

9. LeRoy Hayman, *Harry S. Truman: A Biography* (New York: Crowell, 1969), 127–128.

10. Freidel, *Our Country's Presidents*, 209.

11. Karin C. Farley, *Harry Truman: The Man from Independence* (Englewood Cliffs, N.J.: Messner, 1989), 133.

FURTHER READING

Beard, Charles A. *Charles A. Beard's the Presidents in American History*. Rev. ed. Englewood Cliffs, N.J.: Messner, 1989.

Blassingame, Wyatt. *The Look-It-Up Book of Presidents*. Rev. ed. New York: Random House, 1992.

Blodgett, Bonnie, and J. T. Tice. *At Home with the Presidents*. Woodstock, N.Y.: Overlook Press, 1988.

Blumberg, Rhoda. *First Ladies*. New York: Franklin Watts, 1981.

Cooke, Donald E. *Atlas of the Presidents*. Maplewood, N.J.: Hammond, 1977.

Coy, Harold. *The First Book of Presidents*. Rev. ed. New York: Franklin Watts, 1985.

Cross, Robin. *Roosevelt and the Americans at War*. New York: Franklin Watts, 1990.

Faber, Doris. *Eleanor Roosevelt: First Lady of the World*. New York: Viking Penguin, 1985.

Faber, Doris, and Harold Faber. *Great Lives: American Government*. New York: Scribners, 1988.

Farley, Karin C. *Harry Truman: The Man from Independence*. Englewood Cliffs, N.J.: Messner, 1989.

Feinberg, Barbara Silberdick. *Franklin D. Roosevelt, Gallant President*. New York: Lothrop, Lee and Shepard, 1981.

Fleming, Tom. *Harry S. Truman, President*. New York: Walker, 1993.

Freedman, Russell. *Eleanor Roosevelt: A Life of Discovery*. New York: Clarion Books, 1993.

———. *Franklin Delano Roosevelt*. New York: Clarion Books, 1990.

Garrison, Webb. *A Treasury of White House Tales*. Nashville, Tenn.: Rutledge Hills Press, 1989.

Giblin, James Cross. *Edith Wilson: The Woman Who Ran the United States*. New York: Viking, 1992.

Greenberg, Morrie. *The Buck Stops Here: A Biography of Harry Truman*. Minneapolis: Dillon Press, 1989.

Hargrove, Jim. *Harry S. Truman*. Chicago: Childrens Press, 1987.

Jacobs, David. *An American Conscience: Woodrow Wilson's Search for World Peace*. New York: Harper and Row, 1973.

Kelly, C. Brian. *Best Little Stories from the White House*. Charlottesville, Va.: Montpelier Publishing, 1992.

Larsen, Rebecca. *Franklin D. Roosevelt, Man of Destiny*. New York: Franklin Watts, 1991.

Lindop, Edmund. *Presidents by Accident*. New York: Franklin Watts, 1991.

Melick, Arden Davis. *Wives of the Presidents*. Maplewood, N.J.: Hammond, 1985.

Osinski, Alice. *Franklin D. Roosevelt*. Chicago: Childrens Press, 1987.

———. *Woodrow Wilson*. Chicago: Childrens Press, 1989.

Peare, Catherine Owens. *The Woodrow Wilson Story: An Idealist in Politics*. New York: Crowell, 1963.

Pious, Richard. *The Presidency*. Columbus, Ohio: Silver Burdett, 1991.

Selfridge, John W. *Franklin D. Roosevelt: The People's President*. New York: Fawcett Columbine, 1990.

Shebar, Sharon. *Franklin D. Roosevelt and the New Deal*. Chicago: Childrens Press, 1988.

Stein, R. Conrad. *The Great Depression*. Chicago: Childrens Press, 1993.

———. *The Powers of the President*. Chicago: Childrens Press, 1985.

OTHER SOURCES OF INFORMATION

Alistair Cooke's America: The Arsenal (World War II). Videocassette. Grades 5 and up. BBC/TimeLife Video. Filmic Archives, the Cinema Center, Botsford, CT 06404.

Alistair Cooke's America: The Promise Fulfilled and the Promise Broken (1920s and 1930s). Videocassette. Grades 5 and up. BBC/TimeLife Video. Filmic Archives, the Cinema Center, Botsford, CT 06404.

Basic American History Program 2: Post–Civil War America to the Present. Computer disks for both IBM and Apple. Grades 7 and up. Social Studies School Service, 10200 Jefferson Blvd., P.O. Box 802, Culver City, CA 90232.

The Dawn of the Cold War: Setting the Mold, 1945–1953. Videocassette. Grades 7 and up. Britannica Learning Materials, 310 S. Michigan Ave., Chicago, IL 60604.

D-Day Remembered. Film. Grades 5 and up. National D-Day Museum. The Video Catalog, P.O. Box 64267, St. Paul, MN 55164.

The Eagle and the Bear: U.S.-Soviet Relations Since World War II. Videocassette or 4 filmstrips/4 audiocassettes. Grades 7 and up. Guidance Associates, P.O. Box 3000, Mt. Kisco, NY 10549.

Eleanor Roosevelt: First Lady of the World. Videocassette. Grades 5 and up. National Park Service. National Audiovisual Center, 8700 Edgeworth Drive, Capitol Heights, MD 20743.

F.D.R.—The Man Who Changed America. Film. Grades 7 and up. BFA Educational Media, 468 Park Avenue South, New York, NY 10016.

From Hot to Cold War. Activity book with reproducible pages. Grades 7 and up. Social Science Education Consortium. Social Studies School Service, 10200 Jefferson Blvd., P.O. Box 802, Culver City, CA 90232.

The Great Depression. Film. Grades 5 and up. BFA Educational Media, 468 Park Avenue South, New York, NY 10016.

The Great Depression: A Chronicle of the Lean Years. 2 film-strips/2 audiocassettes. Grades 7 and up. Enrichment. Social Studies School Service,10200 Jefferson Blvd., P.O. Box 802, Culver City, CA 90232.

The Korean War. 5 videocassettes. Grades 7 and up. Korean Broadcast System. The Video Catalog, P.O. Box 64267, St. Paul, MN 55164.

Living American History Series: U.S. History IV (1915–1960). Primary source materials for Apple or IBM computers. Grades 7 and up. Priven Learning Systems. Social Studies School Service, 10200 Jefferson Blvd., P.O. Box 802, Culver City, CA 90232.

The Marshall Plan and Postwar Europe. Videocassette. Grades 7 and up. Random House Media, 400 Hahn Road, Westminster, MD 21157.

Milestone Documents: Roosevelt's "Day of Infamy" Address of 1941. Facsimile of primary source. Grades 6 and up. National Archives. Education Branch, NARA, Washington, DC 20408.

Milestone Documents: Roosevelt's Inaugural Address of 1933. Facsimile of primary source. Grades 6 and up. National Archives. Education Branch, NARA, Washington, DC 20408.

Modern America: The Primary Source, Volume 4. Photocopy masters of primary sources. Grades 7 and up. Perfection Form. Social Studies School Service, 10200 Jefferson Blvd., P.O. Box 802, Culver City, CA 90232.

The New Deal: Witness to History. Videocassette. Grades 5 and up. Guidance Associates, P.O. Box 3000, Mount Kisco, NY 10549.

Normandy: The Great Crusade. CD-ROM for IBM. Grades 5 and up. The Video Catalog, P.O. Box 64267, St. Paul, MN 55164.

Ordeal of a President (Wilson). Videocassette. Grades 5 and up. BFA Educational Media, 468 Park Avenue South, New York, NY 10016.

Pearl Harbor: Surprise Attack! Videocassette. Grades 5 and up. Filmic Archives, the Cinema Center, Botsford, CT 06404.

The Presidents. Videocassette. Grades 7 and up. Post Newsweek Section. Lucerne Media, 37 Ground Pine Road, Morris Plains, NJ 07950.

The Presidents: It All Started with George. CD-ROM for IBM. Grades 5 and up. National Geographic/IBM. National Geographic Educational Services, P.O. Box 98019, Washington, DC 20090.

Roosevelt and U.S. History, 1930–1945. Videocassette. Grades 7 and up. Coronet/MTI Film and Video, 108 Wilmot Road, Deerfield, IL 60015.

Two Great Crusades: 1935–1945 (New Deal and World War II). Videocassette. Grades 5 and up. Filmic Archives, the Cinema Center, Botsford, CT 06404.

U.S. History on CD-ROM. CD-ROM for both IBM and Macintosh. Grades 7 and up. Bureau Development, Inc. Social Studies School Service, 10200 Jefferson Blvd., P.O. Box 802, Culver City, CA 90232.

The United States in World War I: Witness to History. Videocassette. Grades 5 and up. Guidance Associates, P.O. Box 3000, Mount Kisco, NY 10549.

The United States in World War II—The Pacific: Witness to History. Videocassette. Grades 5 and up. Guidance Associates, P.O. Box 3000, Mount Kisco, NY 10549.

Wilson. Videocassette. Grades 5 and up. Twentieth Century Fox.

Baker and Taylor Video, 501 S. Gladiolus, Momence, IL 60954.

Woodrow Wilson: The Fight for a League of Nations. Videocassette. Grades 7 and up. Project 7. Social Studies School Service, 10200 Jefferson Blvd., P.O. Box 802, Culver City, CA 90232.

World War II—The Dark Years in Europe: Witness to History. Videocassette. Grades 5 and up. Guidance Associates, P.O. Box 3000, Mount Kisco, NY 10549.

INDEX